Yosemite

SIMON SPOTLIGHT

An imprint of Simon & Schuster Children's Publishing Division

1230 Avenue of the Americas, New York, New York 10020

This Simon Spotlight edition December 2020

Text copyright © 2020 by Marion Dane Bauer

Illustrations copyright © 2020 by John Wallace
SIMON SPOTLIGHT, READY-TO-READ, and colophon are registered trademarks of Simon & Schuster, Inc.

For information about special discounts for bulk purchases, please contact Simon & Schuster Special Sales at 1-866-506-1949 or business@simonandschuster.com.

Manufactured in the United States of America 1020 LAK

2 4 6 8 10 9 7 5 3 1

Library of Congress Cataloging-in-Publication Data

Names: Bauer, Marion Dane, author. | Wallace, John, illustrator.

Title: Yosemite / by Marion Dane Bauer ; illustrated by John Wallace.

Description: New York, NY : Simon Spotlight, 2020. | Audience: Ages 4-6 | Audience: Grades K-1 | Summary: "Exquisite waterfalls, giant granite cliffs, ample hiking trails, and stunning views—these are just a few of the things that make Yosemite National Park one of the most popular parks in the world. Beginning readers will love exploring and learning about the beauty and grandeur of this iconic park in this informative Ready-to-Read"—Provided by publisher.

Identifiers: LCCN 2020035971 | ISBN 9781534477810 (paperback) | ISBN 9781534477827 (hardcover) | ISBN 9781534477834 (eBook)

Subjects: LCSH: Yosemite National Park (Calif.)—Juvenile literature.

Classification: LCC F868.Y6 B38 2020 | DDC 979.4/47—dc23

LC record available at https://lccn.loc.gov/2020035971

Yosemite

By **Marion Dane Bauer**

Illustrated by **John Wallace**

Ready-to-Read

Simon Spotlight
New York   London   Toronto   Sydney   New Delhi

Would you like to see water
dropping straight down
for almost half a mile?

Yosemite Falls drops 2,425
feet from cliff to valley.

Would you like to see a
waterfall that looks
like fire?

The sun setting on Horsetail
Falls can make it look
like fire.

Do you want to walk among some of the tallest living things on Earth?

Giant sequoia
(say: sih-KWOI-uh)
trees grow in groves
in Yosemite.

Sequoias stand almost as
tall as a football field is long.
Some are more than 3,000
years old.

Would you like to take
a photo of a moonbow?

In bright moonlight,
moonbows appear in
waterfall spray.

You can do all of these
things and more
in Yosemite National Park!

President Abraham Lincoln
signed a bill in 1864 that set aside
this land for the people.
That was before anyone had
thought of national parks.

Today, people go to Yosemite
to hike and to camp.

They go for a chance to see
wild animals like black
bears, bighorn sheep,
and California spotted owls.

They go to climb huge rocks like
Half Dome and El Capitan
(say: EHL kah-pee-TAHN).

They go to the meadows
to see every color of flower.

Or to look for new flowers
like the Yosemite bog orchid
(say: or-KED).

People go to see glaciers just like the glaciers that carved out Yosemite Valley thousands of years ago.

Mainly, they go to be a part
of nature.

Yosemite is ancient,
and it is new every
single day.

So much to see!
So much to do!

Facts About Yosemite

★ People have been living in Yosemite Valley for 8,000 years.

★ Because Yosemite Falls is fed by melted snow, it usually stops flowing in August, when there is little rain and no more melting snow to feed it.

★ Besides the giant sequoias, there are other trees in Yosemite that are very old and grow to a great size. They are the sugar pine, red fir, and ponderosa pine.

★ Years ago, men cut a tunnel through the Wawona Tree (a giant sequoia) so that stagecoaches could drive through. The tree fell after a winter storm in 1969.

★ Half Dome is a widely recognized symbol for Yosemite.

★ El Capitan is a tall monolith (a monolith is a single upright block of stone). El Capitan is one of the most popular rocks to climb.

★ There are hundreds of miles of trails in Yosemite and 3,000 meadows.

★ In the winter many people go to Yosemite to ski.

★ John Muir, a famous naturalist and writer, said of Yosemite, "Only by going alone in silence, without baggage, can one truly get into the heart of the wilderness."